a to z My Body

Beverley Mathias
and
Ruth Thomson

Illustrations: Stephen Iliffe

Franklin Watts
London / New York / Sydney / Toronto

© 1988 Franklin Watts
12a Golden Square
London W1

Franklin Watts Australia
14 Mars Road
Lane Cove
N.S.W. 2066

Franklin Watts Inc
387 Park Avenue South
New York, NY 10016

ISBN: 086313 695 8

Editor: Ruth Thomson
Design: Edward Kinsey

Illustrations © Stephen Iliffe

The authors, illustrator and
Publisher would like to thank the
staff of the Frank Barnes School for
their great help in the preparation
of the Signed English illustrations.

Photographs: Mike Galletly A, B,
D, F, G, H, I, L, M, O, P, S, U; Chris
Fairclough: C, E, K, N, Q, R, T, V,
W, Y, Z; Science Photo Library: X.

Typesetting: Lineage, Watford
Printed in Italy
by *Arti Grafiche* V. Bona S.p.A. - Torino

About this book

* This book has been designed for use by all people learning to read. It is both an information book and a reading book.

* The alphabet is used to provide a natural framework for the exploration of the book's topic and for language development.

* The simple sentences place the key words in context and extend appreciation of the subject.

* The superb photographs have been carefully selected to stimulate interest and discussion.

* The activities that conclude the book are designed to reinforce understanding and to encourage further involvement in the topic.

* A special feature of the book is the provision of Signed English and the Finger Spelling Alphabet for non-hearing readers. This feature is also intended to provide a fascinating introduction to sign language for all readers, teachers and parents.

Beverley Mathias
Ruth Thomson

Aa

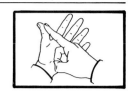

I raise my **arms** in joy.

I raise my arms in joy.

Bb

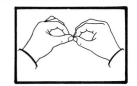

We have our **backs** to you.

We   have   our   backs   to   you.

Cc

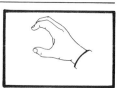

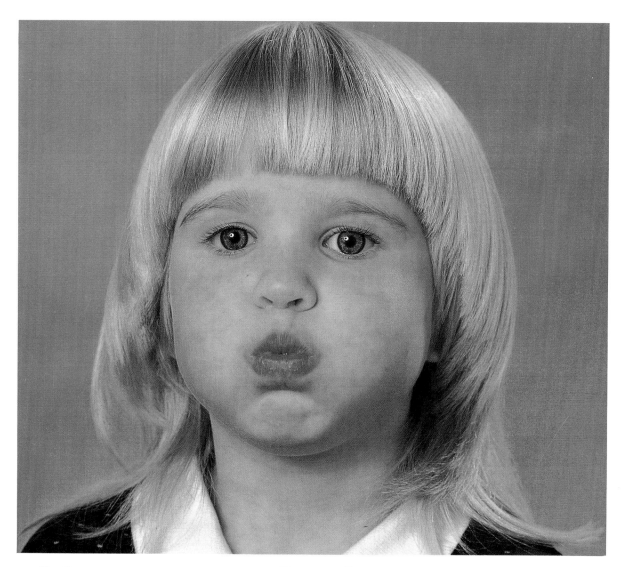

I blow out my cheeks.

I   blow   out   my   cheeks.

Dd

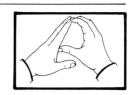

I am in **disguise.**

I   am   in   disguise.

Ee

We see with our **eyes.**

We   see   with   our   eyes.

Ff

Make shapes with your fingers.

Make   shapes   with   your   fingers.

Gg

I need **glasses** to see better.

I   need   glasses   to   see   better.

Hh

Look how long my **hair** is!

Look   how   long   my   hair   is!

Point with your **index** finger.

Point   with   your   index   finger.

Jj

 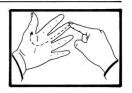

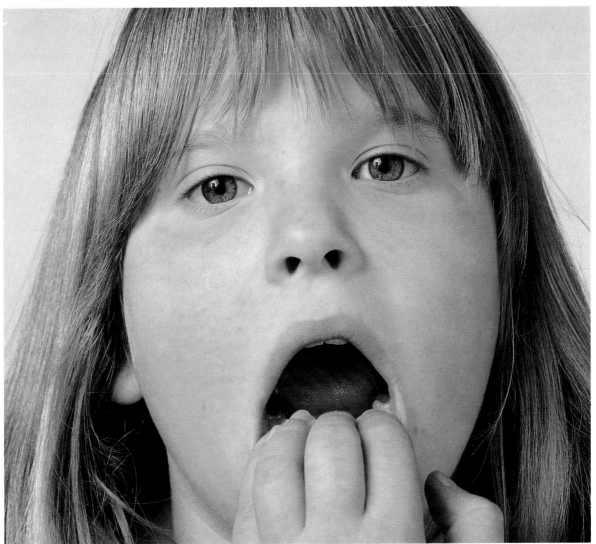

Feel your **jaw** move.

Feel   your   jaw   move.

Kk

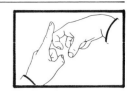

How many **knees** can you see?

How   many   knees   can   you   see?

Ll

We use our **legs** to walk.

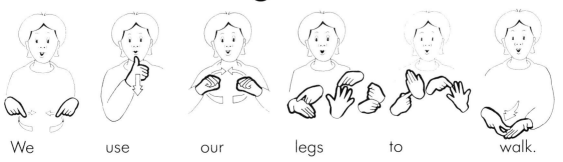

We   use   our   legs   to   walk.

Mm

I eat with my **mouth.**

| I | eat | with | my | mouth. |

Nn

I smell with my **nose.**

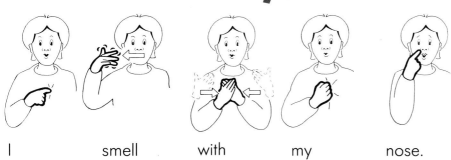

| I | smell | with | my | nose. |

 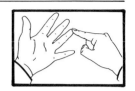

Make an **O** with your mouth.

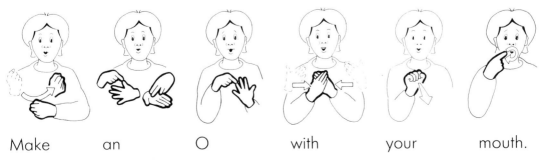

| Make | an | O | with | your | mouth. |

Pp

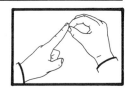

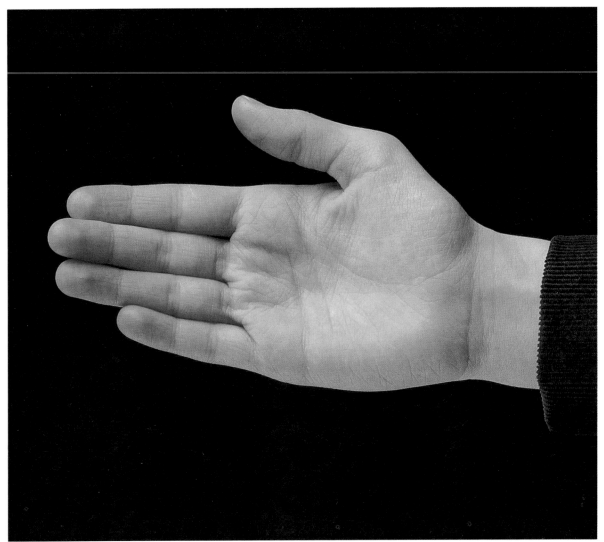

Palms have wrinkles on them.

Palms have wrinkles on them.

Qq

We sit **quietly** in the corner.

We   sit   quietly   in   the   corner.

Rr

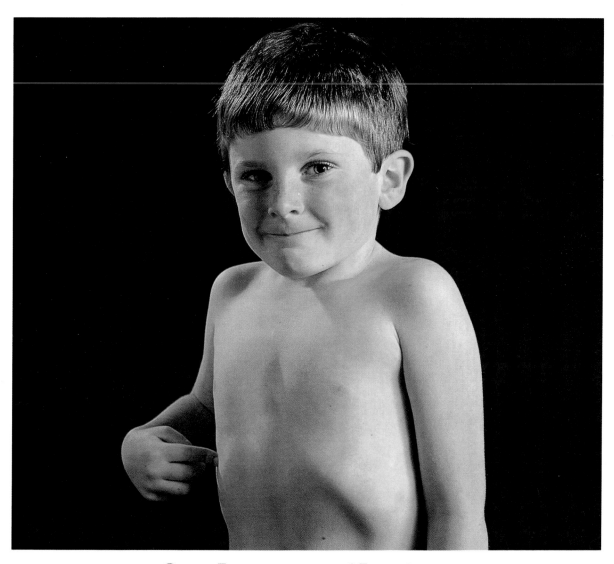

Can you feel your ribs?

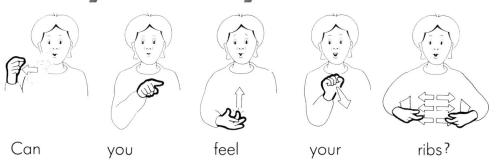

Can you feel your ribs?

Ss

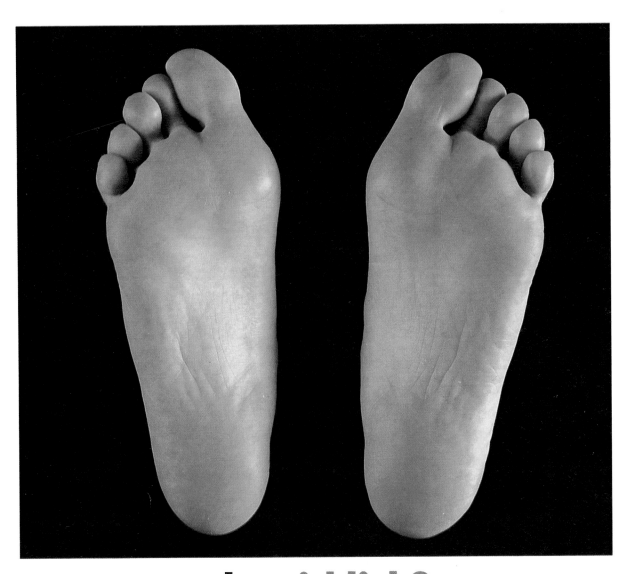

Are your **soles** ticklish?

Are   your   soles   ticklish?

Tt

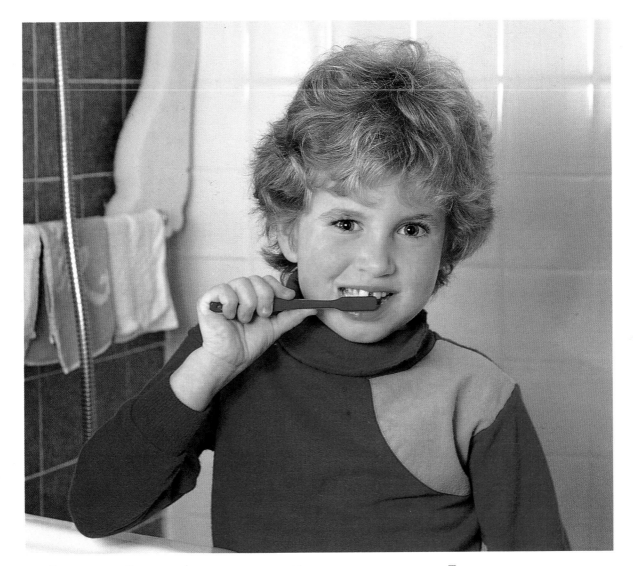

I brush my **teeth** every day.

I   brush   my   teeth   every   day.

Uu

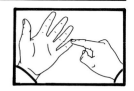

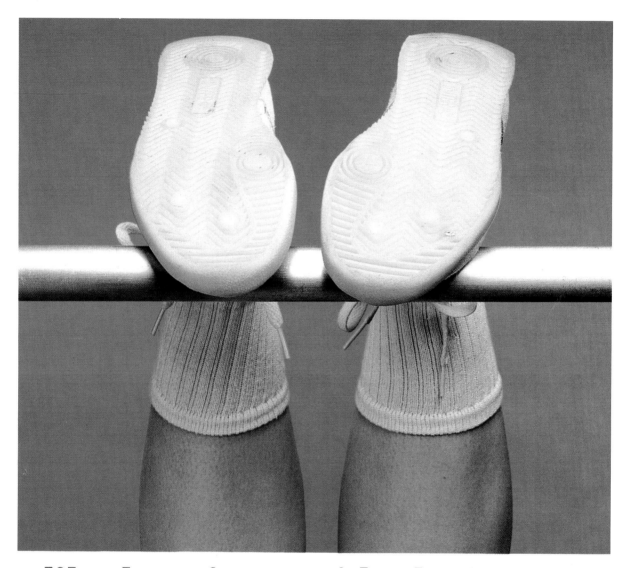

I like hanging upside down.

I   like   hanging   upside down.

Vv

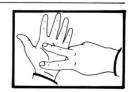

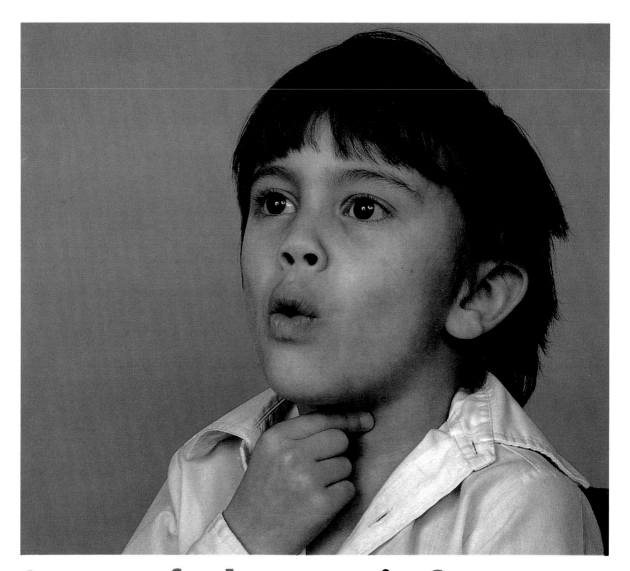

Can you feel your voice?

Can   you   feel   your   voice?

Ww

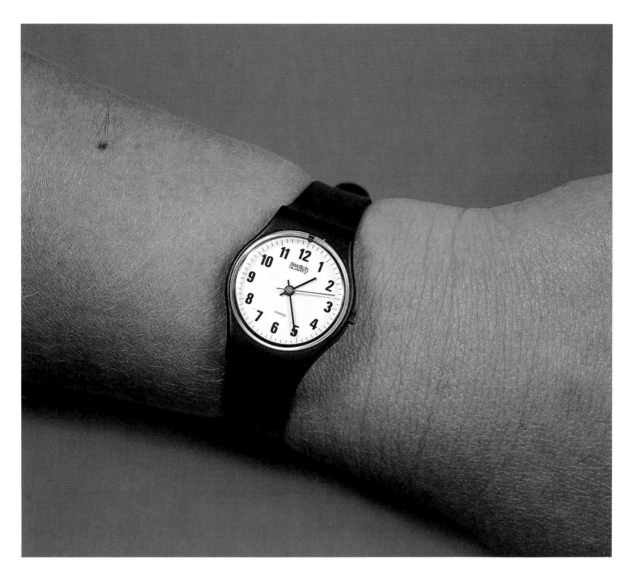

My watch is on my wrist.

My   watch   is   on   my   wrist.

Xx

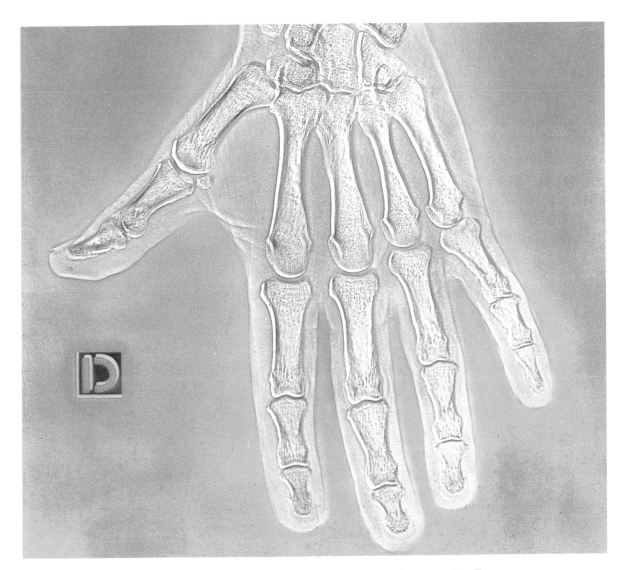

An **X-ray** shows your inside.

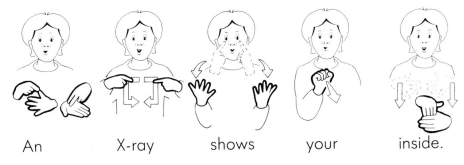

| An | X-ray | shows | your | inside. |

Yy

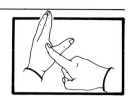

I yawn when I am tired.

I   yawn   when   I   am   tired.

Zz

I am fast asleep. Zzzzz.

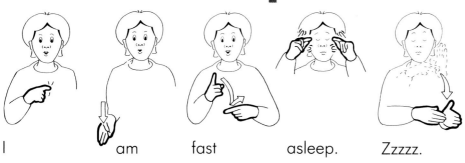

| I | am | fast | asleep. | Zzzzz. |

Label the body

Trace this picture of a person or draw one of your own.
You might even like to make a full size drawing of yourself.
Spread some paper on the floor and lie down on it.
Ask someone to draw round you.

Now see if you can label all the parts.

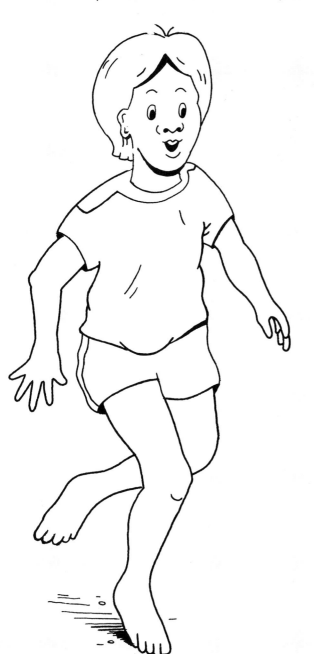

These are some words to help you

head	knee
face	leg
neck	ankle
shoulders	foot
arm	toes
elbow	
wrist	
hand	
fingers	
thumb	
chest	
waist	
tummy	

Now can you make the signs for all these words?

Self-portrait

Now draw a self-portrait of your head and shoulders only.

Label the parts

hair   teeth
forehead   chin
eyebrows   ears
eyes
nose
cheeks
mouth

Simon says

Play this game with a friend or in a group. One player is the caller. He tells the others what to do by saying, for example, 'Simon says, touch your nose' or 'Simon says touch your left knee'.

So long as the caller says 'Simon says do this or that,' everyone else does as he says.

But … if the caller says 'Do this' or 'Do that' without saying 'Simon says' first, then the players stay in their last position.

If a player moves without Simon saying so, that player is out.

The Finger Spelling Alphabet

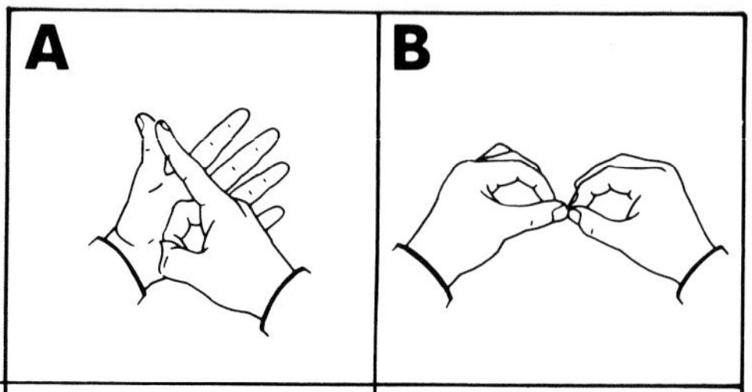

A

B

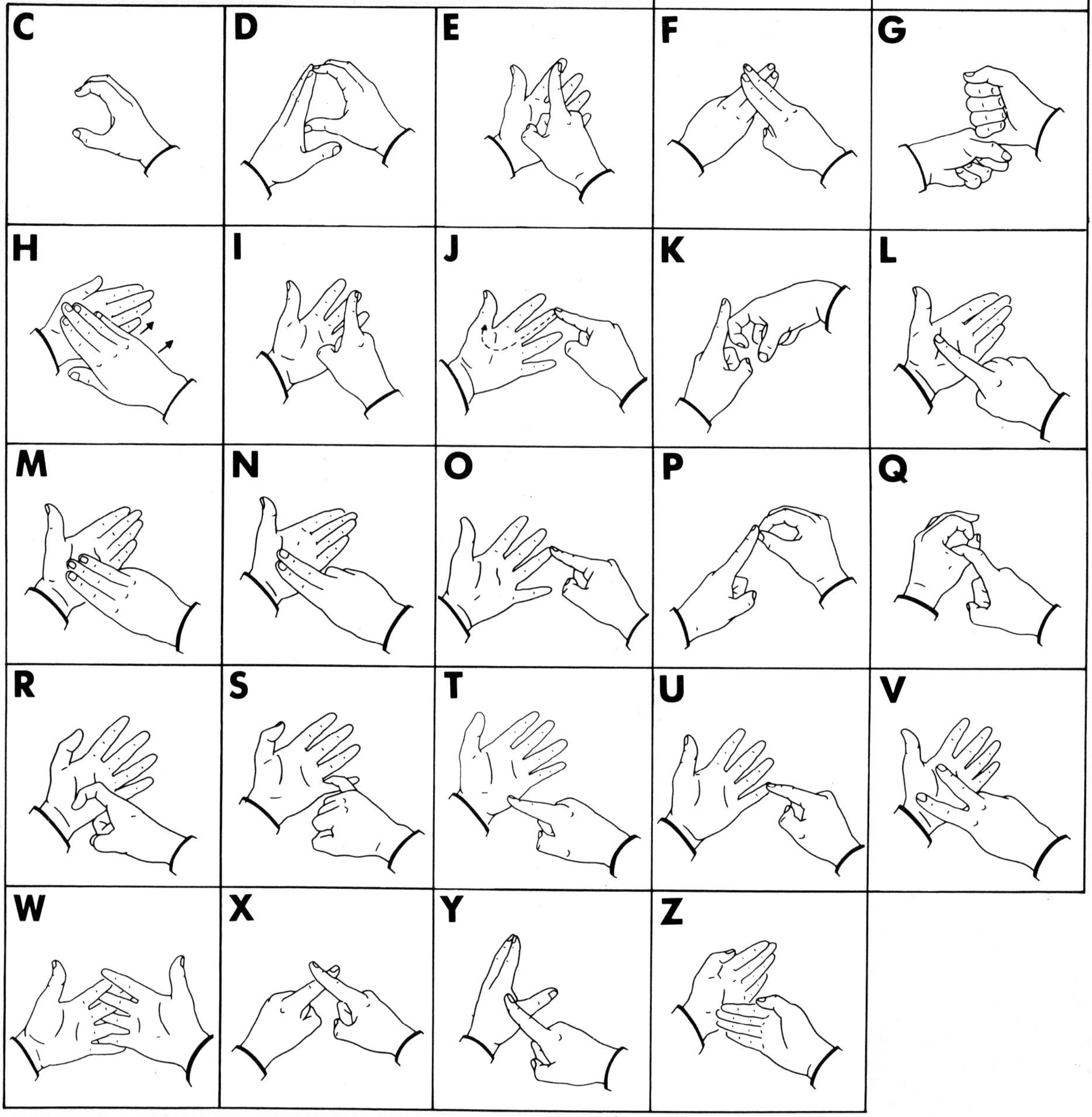

C

D

E

F

G

H

I

J

K

L

M

N

O

P

Q

R

S

T

U

V

W

X

Y

Z